COUNTRIES

# France

Ruth Thomson

## Explore the world with **Popcorn** - your complete first non-fiction library.

Look out for more titles in the Popcorn range. All books have the same format of simple text and striking images. Text is carefully matched to the pictures to help readers to identify and understand key vocabulary. www.waylandbooks.co.uk/popcorn

First published in paperback in 2013 by Wayland


Wayland
Hachette Children's Books
338 Euston Road
London NW1 3BH

Wayland Australia
Level 17/207 Kent Street
Sydney NSW 2000

Produced for Wayland by
White-Thomson Publishing Ltd
www.wtpub.co.uk
+44 (0)843 208 7460



Editor: Steve White-Thomson
Designer: Amy Sparks
Picture researchers: Ruth Thomson/Steve White-Thomson
Series consultant: Kate Ruttle
Design concept: Paul Cherrill

British Library Cataloging in Publication Data
Thomson, Ruth, 1949-
France -- (Countries)(Popcorn)
1. France--Juvenile literature.
I. Title II. Series
914.4-dc22

ISBN: 978 0 7502 7197 4

Wayland is a division of Hachette Children's Books, an Hachette UK company.
www.hachette.co.uk

Printed and bound in China

Picture Credits: Corbis: Stanislas Merlin/cultura front cover; Neil Thomson 23; Photolibrary: Dr Wilfried Bahnmüller 10, Till Jacket/Photononstop 13, Gonzalo Azumendi 15, Gerrit Buntrock 16; Shutterstock: Thierry Maffeis 2/14, Craig Hanson 5, David Hughes 6, bouzou 7, Derek Gordon 8, Vito Zgonc 9, Andreas G. Karelias 11, Phillip Minnis 12, Aaron Amat 15, Marc Pagani Photography 1/18, Sandra van der Steen 20, Christina McWilliams 21

# Contents

# Where is France?

Here is a map of France.
France is the biggest country in western Europe.

Paris is the capital of France. The River Seine flows through the centre.

*The cathedral of Paris is called Nôtre Dame.*

# Land and sea

France has plenty of farmland for growing food crops and feeding animals. It also has forests, hills and high mountains.

**Mont Blanc, in the French Alps, is the highest mountain in Europe.**

*It often rains in the French hills, so the land is very green.*

There are sea coasts in the north, west and south of France. There are many sandy beaches and fishing ports along the coasts.

Fishing boats catch sardines, lobsters, sole and anchovies.

# The weather

Summers are warm in most of France. The south has the hottest and driest summers.

Millions of tourists crowd beaches all over France every summer.

It can be rainy in spring and autumn. In winter, heavy snow falls on the mountains.

People have fun skiing and snowboarding in the Alps during the winter.

# Town and country

Most French people live in towns or cities. In town centres, there are grand old buildings, shops and cafés.

Many town centres are closed to traffic so that people can walk safely.

There are hundreds of small villages and farms dotted across France. Today, fewer people live in the countryside than they did in the past.

**Some country houses have become holiday homes for people who live in towns and cities.**

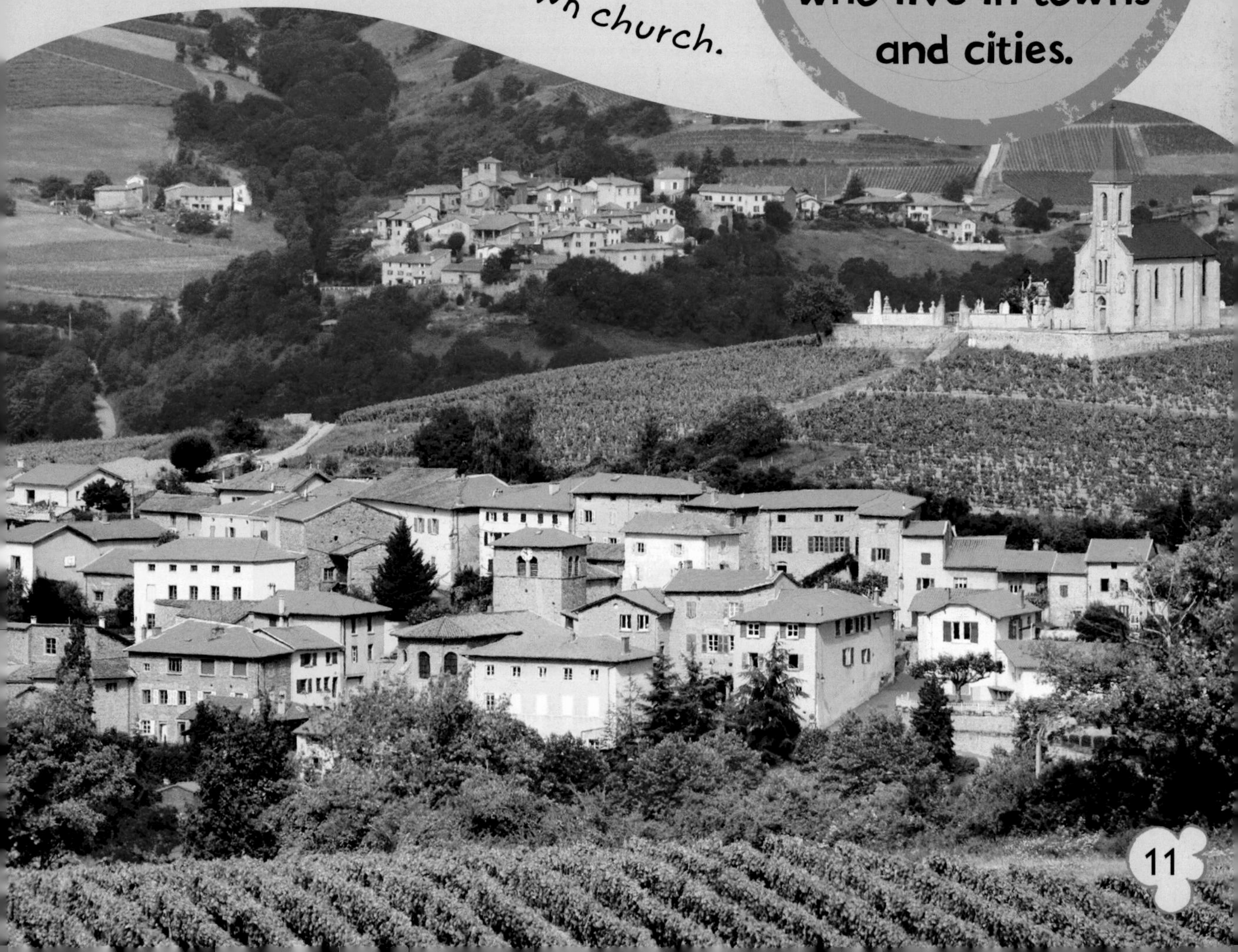

Most villages have their own church.

# Homes

In French towns and cities,
many people live in apartments.
Most apartments have balconies.

*French homes often have window covers called shutters. Can you see them in this photograph?*

Houses in the country usually have gardens. Country people often grow their own vegetables and fruit.

**Some country people keep chickens and rabbits.**

In summer, people pick raspberries and strawberries. In autumn, they pick apples and plums.

# Shopping

People shop for food in supermarkets, the local market and small shops. There are superstores on the edge of cities. Here, people can buy everything they want under one roof.

Markets sell fruit, vegetables and cheese.

Most people buy fresh bread every day from their local bakery. Bakers sell all sorts of loaves and cakes.

The French use euros as their money.

Local bakers have their own bread ovens.

# Food

French people enjoy going to cafés and restaurants. Many families get together for a big meal at weekends.

**The French eat bread with their meals.**

In sunny weather, restaurants put tables outside.

France is famous for its food. These are some typical French foods.

apple tart

oysters

ratatouille (a vegetable stew) from Provence

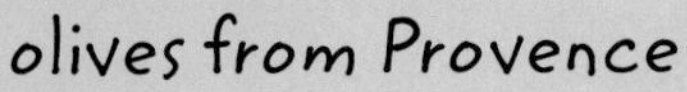

olives from Provence

croissants

cheeses from all over France

# Sport

Football, swimming and cycling are popular sports. Every summer, cyclists race along a route around France.

This race is called the Tour de France.

Many French people are keen on watching football. The national team wears a strip of red, white and blue. These are the colours of the French flag.

France were runners-up to Italy in the 2006 World Cup. They won the World Cup in 1998.

# Holidays and festivals

Most French people stay in France for their holidays. They go to the sea, the country or the mountains. Many families go camping or visit relatives.

People enjoy canoeing on France's many rivers.

July 14 is a national holiday called Bastille Day. People celebrate it with a firework display.

*Paris has the biggest fireworks display in the country. It is held near the Eiffel Tower.*

**The Eiffel Tower has 1,665 steps to the top.**

# Speak French!

| | |
|---|---|
| **Bonjour** *(bon-joor)* | Hello |
| **Comment ça va?** *(kommon sa va?)* | How are you? |
| **Au revoir** *(oh-rev-war)* | Goodbye |
| **S'il vous plait** *(see-voo-play)* | Please |
| **Merci** *(mur-see)* | Thank you |
| **Oui** *(wee)* | Yes |
| **Non** *(nong)* | No |
| **Je m'appelle...** *(jer-map-el)* | My name is... |
| **J'habite** *(jab-ite)* | I live |

The French flag flies on town halls and other public buildings.

# Make a French flag

The French call their flag the tricolore, which means three colours. Blue and red are the colours of Paris and white was once the royal colour.

## You will need:

- plain postcard
- ruler
- red and blue felt-tipped pens
- craft or lolly stick
- glue or sticky tape

1. Measure a postcard width ways. Divide it into three equal parts.

2. Draw a blue line down the left-hand part. Draw a red line down the right-hand part.

3. Colour the left-hand part blue. Colour the right-hand part red.

4. Tape a craft stick on to the back of the flag.

5. You could use your flag as a decoration or as a bookmark.

# Glossary

**apartment** a home with rooms all on the same level of a building

**balcony** a platform on the outside of a building with railings or a wall around it

**capital** the city in a country where the government is

**cathedral** the main church in a city

**flag** a piece of cloth with a pattern on it. Every country has a different flag.

**market** a place with stalls where people buy and sell things

**port** a town by the sea with a harbour for boats

**superstore** a huge self-service shop that sells all sorts of goods

**tourist** someone who travels for fun or on holiday

# Index